United States
Department of
Agriculture

Forest Service

Pacific Northwest
Research Station

General Technical
Report
PNW-GTR-827
August 2010

Developing Estimates of Potential Demand for Renewable Wood Energy Products in Alaska

Allen M. Brackley, Valerie Barber, and Cassie Pinkel

The **Forest Service** of the U.S. Department of Agriculture is dedicated to the principle of multiple use management of the Nation's forest resources for sustained yields of wood, water, forage, wildlife, and recreation. Through forestry research, cooperation with the States and private forest owners, and management of the National Forests and National Grasslands, it strives—as directed by Congress—to provide increasingly greater service to a growing Nation.

The U.S. Department of Agriculture (USDA) prohibits discrimination in all its programs and activities on the basis of race, color, national origin, age, disability, and where applicable, sex, marital status, familial status, parental status, religion, sexual orientation, genetic information, political beliefs, reprisal, or because all or part of an individual's income is derived from any public assistance program. (Not all prohibited bases apply to all programs.) Persons with disabilities who require alternative means for communication of program information (Braille, large print, audiotape, etc.) should contact USDA's TARGET Center at (202) 720-2600 (voice and TDD). To file a complaint of discrimination, write USDA, Director, Office of Civil Rights, 1400 Independence Avenue, SW, Washington, DC 20250-9410 or call (800) 795-3272 (voice) or (202) 720-6382 (TDD). USDA is an equal opportunity provider and employer.

Authors

Allen M. Brackley is a research forester, U.S. Department of Agriculture, Forest Service, Pacific Northwest Research Station, Alaska Wood Utilization Research and Development Center, 204 Siginaka Way, Sitka, AK 99835; **Valerie A. Barber** is a research scientist, University of Alaska Fairbanks, Cooperative State Research, Education, and Extension Service, Forest Products Program, Palmer Research and Extension Service, 533 E Fireweed Avenue, Palmer, AK 99645; and **Cassie Pinkel** is a project manager, Fairbanks Economic Development Corporation, 301 Cushman Street, Suite 301, Fairbanks, AK 99701.

Cover photographs by David Nicholls.

Abstract

Brackley, Allen M.; Barber, Valerie A.; Pinkel, Cassie. 2010. Developing estimates of potential demand for renewable wood energy products in Alaska. Gen. Tech. Rep. PNW-GTR-827. Portland, OR: U.S. Department of Agriculture, Forest Service, Pacific Northwest Research Station. 31 p.

Goal three of the current U.S. Department of Agriculture, Forest Service strategy for improving the use of woody biomass is to help develop and expand markets for woody biomass products. This report is concerned with the existing volumes of renewable wood energy products (RWEP) that are currently used in Alaska and the potential demand for RWEP for residential and community heating projects in the state. In this report, data published by the U.S. Department of Commerce, Bureau of Census and the U.S. Department of Energy, Energy Information Agency have been used to build a profile of residential and commercial energy demand for Alaska census tracts. By using peak prices from the fall of 2008, the potential value of a British thermal unit (Btu) from various fuels has been calculated to identify those situations where wood-based fuels are economically competitive or advantageous when compared with alternative fuel sources. Where these situations are identified, the Btu usage has been converted to equivalent volumes of wood energy products. Data have been presented so potential demand is available by census tract. No attempt has been made to define the rate of conversion or the time that it will take for total conversion to renewable wood energy. The ultimate rate of conversion is a function of government policies that encourage conversion, costs associated with converting, and price of alternative fuels. If fuel oil prices increase to the levels experienced in 2008, there would be a strong economic incentive to convert heating systems to use solid wood fuels. If all of the liquid fuels used by the residential and commercial sectors in Alaska were converted to solid wood energy, it is estimated that 1.3 million cords of material would be required annually.

Keywords: Alaska, wood energy, heating fuels.

Contents

Introduction

The current U.S. Department of Agriculture, Forest Service strategy for improving the use of woody biomass (Patton-Mallory 2008) defines four strategy goals. Goals one, two, and four include building partnerships, developing and deploying science and technology, and assuring a supply of biomass. Goal three of the strategy is to "help develop new and expanded markets for bioenergy and biobased products" (Patton-Mallory 2008: 8). All goals are viewed by the Forest Service as important parts of a primary and broader objective of sustaining healthy forests that will survive natural disturbances and threats, including climate change.

A planned short-term action of goal three is to "assist businesses looking to develop new markets or increase the supply of woody biomass products, particularly focused on heating fuels such as pellets and wood chips or commercial use and long-life products that maintain sequestered carbon" (Patton-Mallory 2008: 9). Accordingly, the purpose of this project was to better define the existing profile of heating fuels used in various areas of the state of Alaska and identify opportunities to replace higher cost fossil fuels with renewable wood energy products (RWEP). The need for the estimates of potential markets became noticeable as forest managers, entrepreneurs, civic officials, and citizens expressed increasing interest in using various forms of local biomass directly as sources of energy or for production of energy products (traditional firewood, wood pellets, briquettes, and chips). Although supply was a primary concern, it was assumed that if the material existed, it could be delivered and made available.

Markets, price, and the sources of existing competing energy are all important considerations. Given the high transportation costs to import products to Alaska, local markets and levels of demand are important components of any business plan to produce energy products. Local producers may have a competitive transportation advantage when serving local markets owing to lower transportation costs than those faced by a competitor producing outside the region. It is not uncommon, however, for this competitive advantage in transportation costs to be offset by higher production costs in Alaska. Regardless, the size of the local market and potential demand are of critical importance to firms, organizations, and entrepreneurs interested in production and marketing renewable energy products in Alaska.

There are many factors that will influence the conversion from traditional fossil fuels to RWEPs. Nicholls et al. (2009) reviewed opportunities for the increased use of bioenergy, or RWEP, in the Western United States. They reviewed the legislation and policies that some European nations have adopted to promote conversion and maximum use of RWEP. There are many other factors exterior to government policy that also impact the conversion process in any community or region in the

> A planned short-term action of goal three is to "assist businesses looking to develop new markets or increase the supply of woody biomass products.

Nation. These include availability of various fuels at the local level; the local cost of the alternative fuels; replacement costs of heating equipment; environmental regulations at the community, state, and federal levels; the existing forest products industry and level of activity; and carbon accounting and environmental economics. A complete analysis of all these problems is beyond the scope of this project. The goal of this project is to provide estimates of the potential demand for RWEP in Alaska, and provide sufficient background material so the reader can begin to estimate the required raw material to meet that demand.

Objectives

The Alaska Wood Utilization Research and Development Center has a mandate to conduct projects that have the potential to more efficiently utilize the forest resources of Alaska and to promote the economic development of the state. The methodology employed in this project also has the potential to provide researchers with a model that can be applied to any area of the Nation.

The objectives of the project are as follows:

- Provide an overview of the conversion factors and measurement methods— using data generally available from the U.S. Department of Commerce, Bureau of the Census; U.S. Department of Energy, Energy Information Agency (EIA); and other sources, primarily Fairbanks Economic Development Corporation (FEDC)—to compare forms of energy used in the residential and commercial sectors of various geographic regions in Alaska. Special emphasis is placed on measurement and recoverable energy from RWEP, often referred to as biomass products.
- Using Census Bureau, EIA, and FEDC data, estimate the volumes of renewable wood energy that are currently used in Alaska as a primary or secondary fuel for heating purposes.
- Compare the cost per British thermal unit (Btu) of the various alternative sources of energy used in Alaska, and identify situations where renewable wood energy is an economically viable replacement for existing sources of energy.
- Develop estimates of the total volume of renewable wood energy required to replace high-cost alternatives in the residential and commercial sectors in Alaska.

Overview of Methods to Compare Energy Use

There are three major categories of biomass or RWEP: (1) trees harvested specifically for energy (stem or bowl wood limbs, needles, and leaves—including species that will grow under intensive forestry methods), (2) wood fiber residue from sawmills and other plants that process timber (these residues include coarse or chippable residue, sawdust, planer shavings, and bark), and (3) tops and limbs (from trees harvested for traditional products) that are processed in the woods or removed from the woods and converted to energy use. When used for energy, these forms of wood fiber can be burned as is; hogged prior to burning; processed into pellets, compressed logs, or bricks; or as technology improves, manufactured into liquid forms such as biodiesel and ethanol. The focus of this project is the near-term replacement of fossil fuels by the solid forms of RWEP.

Conversion Factors in This Report

The basic energy content of RWEP is reported as Btu values. British thermal unit values are determined by using various calorimeters charged with bone-dry (zero percent moisture content) material and reported in the English system on the basis of weight (Wilson et al. 1987). The standard methods for determining species-specific Btu ratings result in a value referred to as the higher heating value (HHV), or laboratory value, for the material (Briggs 1994, Ince 1979). The reported standard Btu values for wood (Wilson et al. 1987) from the Pacific Northwest extends from a low of about 8,000 Btu/lb (red alder (*Alnus rubra* Bong.))[1] to a high of 9,900 Btu/lb (Alaska yellow-cedar (*Chamaecyparis nootkatensis* (D. Don) Spach)). These values are relatively constant.

Higher heating values for Alaska species used as fuel are presented in table 1. Using the Wilson et al. (1987) values for nine species that grow in Alaska, an average value for species in the state was calculated as 8,653 Btu/lb. The standard deviation of these values was 571 Btu/lb. The energy value for bark is generally higher than that for wood. Based on this information, the HHV of Alaska wood for the purposes of this analysis is 8,500 Btu/lb. Table 2 contains HHV for other fuels derived from data reported by the EIA (2008d). For wood fuel, the EIA uses a factor of 20 million Btu per cord. For biomass (wood and wood-derived fuels), the EIA uses a factor of 17.2 million Btu per short ton, based on zero moisture content.

The focus of this project is the near-term replacement of fossil fuels by the solid forms of renewable wood energy products.

---

[1] See "Common and Scientific Names" for species names used in this paper.

Table 1—Higher heating values for wood and bark for species growing in Alaska[a]

Species	Wood	Bark	Percentage of bark by volume
	British thermal units per oven-dry pound		*Percent*
Alaska yellow-cedar	9,900	—	11–13.1
Black cottonwood	8,800	8,882	18.3
Paper birch	8,334	9,900	8–15.7
Quaking aspen	8,200[b]	8,571	8.9–16.5
Red alder	7,995	8,583	13.5
Sitka spruce	8,100	—	—
Western hemlock	8,515	9,421	6.3–16.3
Western redcedar	9,144	8,854	5–13
White spruce	8,890	8,626	8.6–11.7
Average value	8,653	8,977	
Standard deviation	571		

— = no data available.

[a] Some values are shown as the average of the range listed in the source.

[b] This value was obtained by adjusting the value given in air dry condition to oven dry.

Source: Wilson et al. 1987.

Table 2—Higher heating value factors used by the Energy Information Administration (EIA) to calculate reported British thermal unit (Btu) values of selected fuels

Fuel	Btu per barrel	Btu per gallon[a]	Btu per cubic foot	Btu per cord[b]	Btu per short ton[c]	Btu per kilowatt-hour
	Million		*Thousand*	*Million*	*Million*	
Biomass[d]					17.2	
Coal/coke					15.6	
Distillate	5.825	138,690				
Electricity						3,412[e]
Kerosene	5.670	135,000				
Liquefied petroleum gas	3.620	86,190				
Motor gasoline	5.218	124,238				
Natural gas			1.030			
Wood				20.0		

[a] 42 gallons per barrel.

[b] The cord is a unit of volume that is constant over a wide range of moisture content values. As the moisture content is reduced, the weight of the cord is also reduced while the gross heating value (GHV) per unit of wood weight increases. Total Btu available from the wood is a function of the GHV × weight of wood.

[c] Recoverable Btu are relatively constant over a range of moisture contents for the volume. A Btu value per ton of 17.2 million is based on a bone-dry moisture content (zero moisture content).

[d] Biomass is organic nonfossil material of biological origin constituting a renewable energy source. The EIA defines biomass as "wood and wood-derived fuels."

[e] The Btu per kilowatt-hour conversion is based on the International Units of 3,412.14.

Source: EIA 2008d.

Wood Measurement and Fuel Characteristics

Currently, most wood transported on the highways to forest product facilities is commonly purchased and sold based on fresh cut (green) weight. The cord, however, is still a common unit of measure used to define volumes of wood that are purchased and sold at the retail level for home heating purposes. Numerous sources and forest mensuration texts (Bruce and Schumacher 1950, Evans 2000, Husch et al. 1982) define a cord as a pile of wood, with lengths cut to 4 ft, that has a volume of 128 ft^3 (4 ft high × 4 ft wide × 8 ft long). The unit is further defined as a pile of wood that includes wood, bark, and void air space. The older text (Bruce and Schumacher 1950) was written when the cord unit was a commonly used measure for pulpwood and firewood. This text stated, "There may be anywhere from 60 to 100 cu. ft. of solid wood per cord, depending on the mentioned circumstances" (Bruce and Schumacher 1950: 35). They continued, "Where an average figure is needed, 90 may be considered high and 70 a low, value..." Keep in mind that a cord of wood also includes bark. The exact amount of bark available for burning is a function of species characteristics, time of year the material is processed, handling, and time between harvest and burning. Energy of burnable material may be increased up to 10 percent if all bark is delivered to the stove. Thus, a cord with a wood content of 85 ft^3 would be the equivalent of 93.5 ft^3 when bark is included.

Newer sources (Dunster and Dunster 1996) also make reference to a "face cord" and note that this is material that is cut to usable lengths (12, 16, or 24 in) and, when split for burning and piled, has a face area of 32 ft^2 (or 4 ft high and 8 ft long). A face cord of 24-in material would contain one-half the volume of a standard cord, all other variables being equal.

The previous paragraphs start to identify some of the problems incurred when energy values derived on a weight basis are applied to a product that is measured by volume. The previous comments are concerned with the problems of measuring the unit volume, but the magnitude of the problem becomes clearer when the weight-based energy values of the material are applied to volumes.

A review of the USDA Forest Service wood handbook (USDA FS 1999) indicates that the reported green specific gravity of the wood species (softwoods and hardwoods) that grow in the United States range from a low of 0.29 to a high of 0.66 (USDA FS 1999: table 4-3b). Conversion of these values to density results in values that range from a low of 18.1 lb to a high of 41.2 lb of green wood per cubic foot of wood material. A similar review of specific gravity values for material at 12 percent moisture content shows that the specific gravity of this relatively dry material ranges from 0.31 to 0.75, or a range of density from 19.3 to 46.8 lb/ft^3. Note that green material will shrink when dried below fiber saturation point and will have less volume, but the impact of this volume change is minimal when compared with the natural variation in cord weights composed of various species. In the above comments relative to Btu values, it was noted that for the purposes of this report, all RWEP would be assigned an HHV rating of 8,500 Btu/lb. Once this starting point was established, the next step required to calculate the recoverable Btu of a heating system was to adjust for fuel moisture content (Briggs 1994, Ince 1979). This calculation takes into account the energy that is required to drive off the water during the combustion process.

The moisture content of fresh-cut wood differs considerably among species (Bowyer et al. 2003). In general, the heartwood is of lower moisture content than the sapwood. As a rule of thumb, many consultants assume that fresh-cut wood is half (50 percent) water. Wood is hydroscopic in nature, and it gains and looses moisture with the surrounding environment. In most coastal areas of Alaska, green wood, stored so that it is covered from the rain and piled so that air will circulate through the material, will dry to an equilibrium moisture content of 15 to 16 percent, green basis. Inland areas will reach equilibrium at slightly lower levels. Drying rates of Sitka spruce (*Picea sitchensis* (Bong.) Carr.) and western hemlock (*Tsuga heterophylla* (Raf.) Sarg.) logs were reported by Nicholls and Brackley (2009). Regardless, in situations where older heating equipment is used, wood at the stated equilibrium moisture contents may create unacceptable levels of emissions and exceed Environmental Protection Agency (EPA) emission standards (ECFR 2009). The problem may be especially acute during periods of temperature inversion, which happens frequently in the winter in Fairbanks and Juneau, the second and third largest cities in Alaska. In more urban areas of Alaska, local ordinance may require heating equipment that meets EPA emission standards or limits the use of older stoves during certain weather conditions.

Most moisture content values in the Forest Service wood handbook (USDA FS 1999) are based on the dry weight of the wood (dry basis). In energy applications, adjustments for moisture content are based on the original green weight of the material (green basis). The following formula allows conversion from dry to green basis when the values are expressed as a percentage (Kollman and Cote 1968):

$$MC_{db} = (100 \times MC_{gb}) / (100 - MC_{gb}) \text{ or}$$

$$MC_{gb} = (100 \times MC_{db}) / (100 + MC_{db}),$$

where

MC_{db} = moisture content, dry basis expressed as a percentage, and

MC_{gb} = moisture content, green basis expressed as a percentage.

> As a rule of thumb, many consultants assume that fresh-cut wood is half (50 percent) water.

Once a moisture content of 12 percent dry basis is adjusted to 10.7 percent green basis, the equation presented by Briggs (1994) or Ince (1979) can be used to calculate gross heating value (GHV) when burning takes place, using the following formula:

$$GHV = HHV \times (1 - [MC_{gb} / 100]),$$

where

GHV = gross heating value,

HHV = higher heating value, and

MC_{gb} = moisture content, green basis expressed as a percentage.

Thus, the HHV value of 8,500 Btu/lb for wood material adjusted using the above formula (with MC_{gb} equal to 10.7) will produce a GHV of 7,590 Btu/lb. When the range of cubic-foot weights (19.3 to 46.8 lb/ft^3) are applied to the calculated GHV value, the GHV of a cubic foot of wood ranges from a low of 146,487 Btu/ft^3 to a high of 355,212 Btu/ft^3. Cords represent volume that is expressed in terms of cubic feet.[2] In this analysis, we have considered volumes that have been reduced to a moisture content of 10.7 percent green basis. If the analysis were repeated and values of GHV at higher moisture contents included, the range would more than double. This analysis is intended to demonstrate some of the problems of assigning weight-based energy HHV values to any volume-related factor. The bottom line is to always start the process with weight values and then make the conversion to volume in the final stages. When the final conversion from weight to volume is made, always provide the factor for the conversion.

Up until this point, the focus of energy recovery has been on the characteristics of the fuel. Ultimately, the final calculations to determine the recoverable heat and combustion efficiency of any heating system must also take into consideration the equipment that is used and the insulation of the building that is being heated.

Efficiency of heating systems—

In any heating system, the energy from the combustion process is either vented up the chimney (stack heat loss), lost to the environment during transfer to the area being heated, or applied to the area being heated. The direct transfer of heat (energy) may be by a process, singularly or in combination, of radiation and convection. Both Briggs (1994) and Ince (1979) provided formulas for converting GHV values to recoverable heat or combustion efficiency values.

In any heating system, the energy from the combustion process is either vented up the chimney (stack heat loss), lost to the environment during transfer to the area being heated, or applied to the area being heated.

---

[2] The EIA (2008d) value for wood in table 2 (20 million Btu/cord) can be converted to 235,294 Btu/ft^3 (assuming 85 ft^3 per cord).

The product and marketing literature for space heating stoves (regardless of fuel type), furnaces, water heaters, and other appliances include an efficiency rating expressed as a combustion efficiency value. Most modern wood heating units also include an EPA-based emissions rating. The standards that products must meet are defined by the National Appliance Energy Conservation Act (NAECA 1987) and Department of Energy regulations. Technically, the efficiency rating reported by Briggs (1994) is comparable to the ratings reported for various heating stoves under the NAECA. Some sources present tables where HHV values for various systems are reduced by the efficiency rating of the equipment to obtain estimates of combustion efficiency or deliverable Btus for various fuels. The results of this approach are reasonable for simple systems using most liquid fuels with minor or low moisture contents. They do not, however, provide reasonable estimates for fuels such as wood, many RWEP, and Alaska coal with high moisture contents. Gross heating values reduced by appliance efficiency are probably optimistic and higher than most installations, given that stove testing is done under optimal conditions where stack properties and air feeds are controlled. The installation of the product in less controlled conditions of a specific home will probably result in a combustion efficiency value lower than that reported by the manufacturer.

Impact of climate on home heating—
From north to south, the state of Alaska is a distance of about 1,000 mi. Within the state, the mean annual heating degree days using a base of 65 °F, range from a low of 6,855 at Annette Island in southeast Alaska to a high of 19,719 degree days in Kuparuk, a community on Prudhoe Bay in northern Alaska (ACRC 2009). Degree days provide a rough estimate of heating requirements. The values may not, however, be directly correlated to energy use for heating, unless the characteristics of housing units (size of heated living area, amount of insulation, efficiency of heating systems, etc.) in each location are taken into consideration. A poorly insulated house in a warmer area with fewer degree days may require more energy for heating than a well-insulated house in a colder area with more degree days.

> A poorly insulated house in a warmer area with fewer degree days may require more energy for heating than a well-insulated house in a colder area with more degree days.

Review of U.S. Census Bureau Data

The federal government conducts a census every 10 years to determine the apportionment of congressional representatives among states. Although the government collects the data for apportionment, distribution of federal funds, delineation of legislative districts, and other purposes, the information is also available to the general public and businesses. The information is especially valuable to businesses for use in marketing applications.

As stated in the objectives, one purpose of this project is to review the current profile of energy used to heat residential homes and commercial businesses in Alaska. An important statistic for use in this activity is housing units in census tracts.

Currently, the methods for collecting census housing information are in a state of flux as the Census Bureau converts from periodic to continuous systems of data collection (U.S. Census Bureau 2000, 2004, 2005a, 2006a). During the transition period, updated estimates of the total number of housing units in Alaska (or any state) are available for 2006, but many of the tables for census tracts are not updated to reflect these changes. For the purposes of this project, updated census tract housing totals for 2006 have been used to update the original 2000 table, based on the assumption that change in all units is proportional. This adjustment required minimal effort and allowed the authors to proceed with preliminary calculations relative to local demand and may have induced minor but insignificant errors in the final results.

A map showing the location of Alaska census tracts is presented in figure 1.

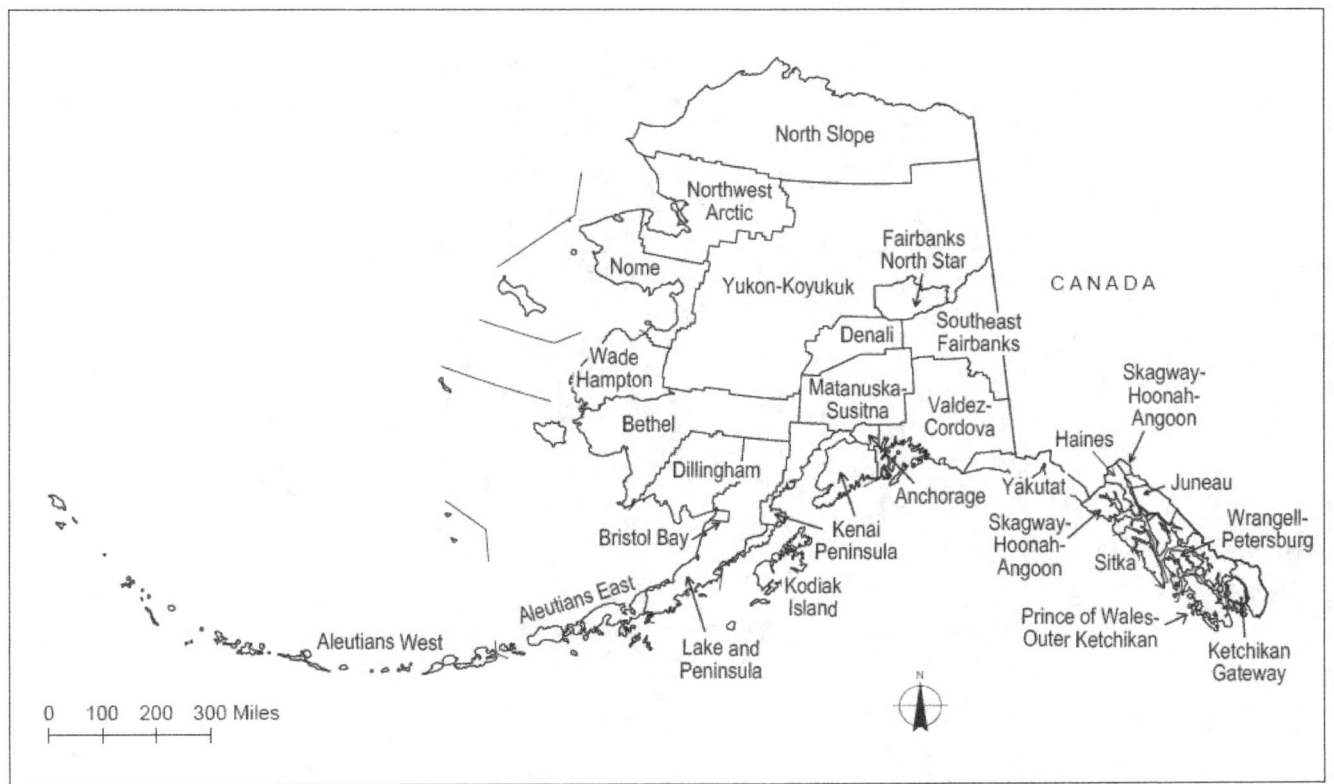

Figure 1—Alaska census tracts (U.S. Census Bureau 2005b).

Natural gas (45 percent) is the primary fuel used for home heating in Alaska, and wood is used for heat in 4 percent of the homes.

The American Community Survey (U.S. Census Bureau 2006a) also collects information relative to home living area, unit age, occupancy, and home ownership. In the following sections, the above data may be modified to reflect estimates of occupied homes, owner-occupied homes, or other factors. Such modifications have been noted as they appear. The profile of energy sources used for home heating on a household basis in Alaska from the Census Bureau sources are presented in figure 2. It shows that natural gas (45 percent) is the primary fuel used for home heating in Alaska, and wood is used for heat in 4 percent of the homes.

Review of Energy Information Agency Data

The EIA State Energy Data System (SEDS) reports energy consumption estimates for each state. The basic data on energy sources (EIA 2008a, 2008b) are reported in terms of Btu values and units of sale used in the commerce of the United States. The conversion factors used to calculate Btu are reported in the technical notes and documentation to SEDS (EIA 2008d). The information (EIA 2008a) is reported for

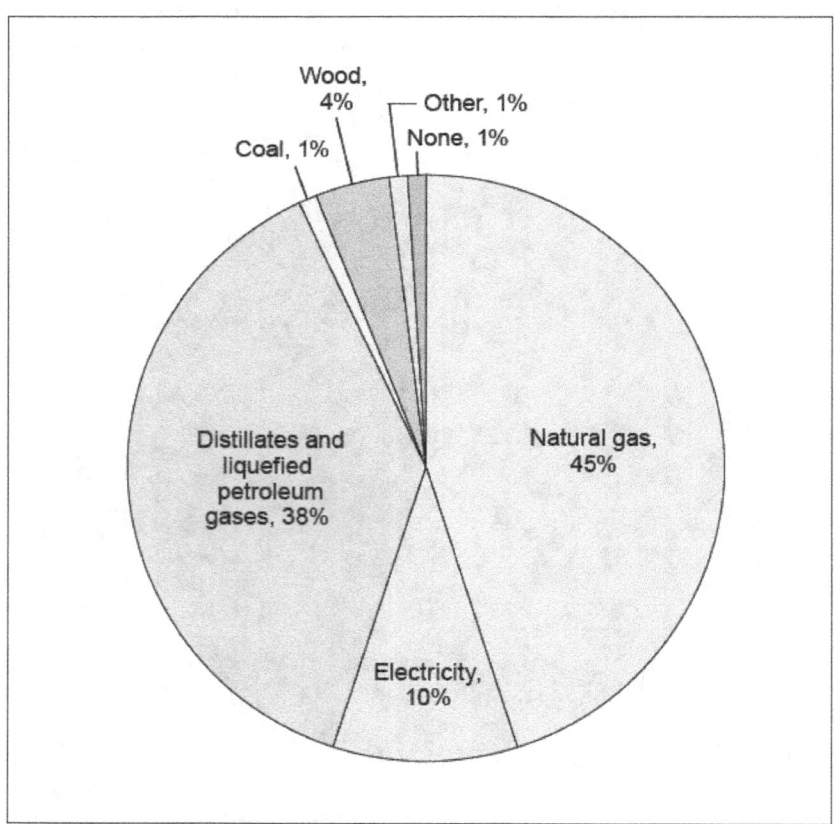

Figure 2—Fuel used as primary source for home heating in Alaska (2005) based on number of reported housing units by Bureau of Census 2000 (U.S. Census Bureau 2000, 2005a, 2006b).

the following sectors of the economy: residential, commercial, industrial, transportation, and electric power. The profile of Btu usage for Alaska's residential sector based on EIA energy sources are reported in figure 3. The overall breakdown is similar to that shown in figure 2, with natural gas having the highest percentage (46) and biomass (or wood and wood-derived fuels) at 7 percent.

The EIA data (fig. 3) report the energy profile for all residential uses (heating, appliances operation, lighting, and others). The Census Bureau data (fig. 2) report the profile for heating based on number of households. The definition used by EIA to define the residential sector does not correspond directly with the Census Bureau-defined sector. The major difference between the two classification systems is that EIA considers multiunit apartment buildings as part of the commercial sector, whereas the Census Bureau considers these units as part of the residential component. Given the rural nature of Alaska, however, it is considered a minor problem.

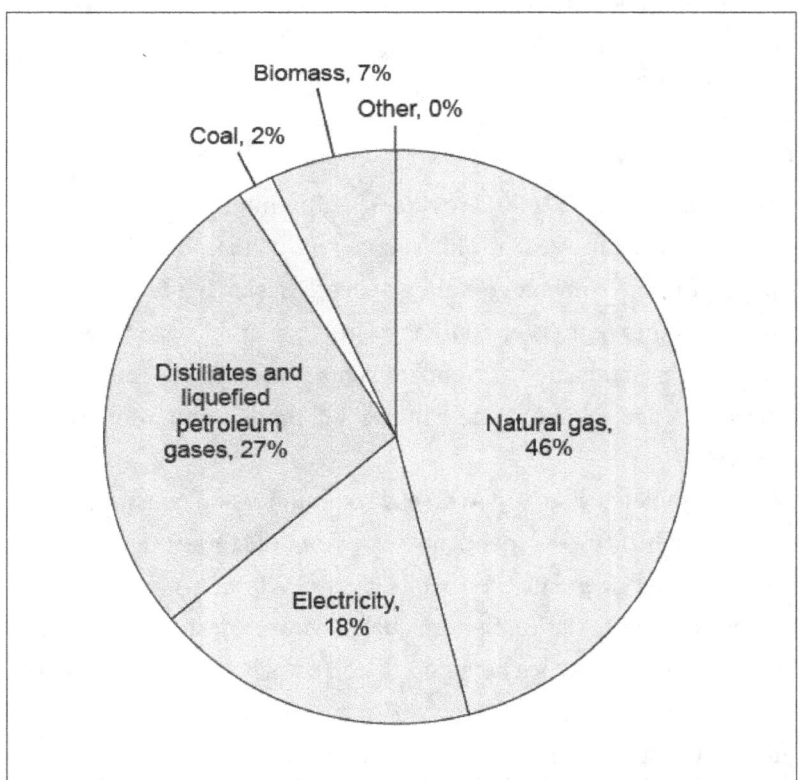

Figure 3—Energy use in the residential sector of Alaska (2005) based on British thermal unit values. Biomass includes wood and wood-derived fuels (EIA 2008a).

Table 3 presents the profile of energy use for Alaska. With respect to forms of fuel used, the Alaska energy profile can be characterized as one where over twice the volume of natural gas (54.3 percent vs. 22.6 percent) and less than one-tenth the volume of coal (1.8 percent vs. 22.7 percent) are used compared to national averages (EIA 2008a). The energy profile also shows that an unusually high percentage of jet fuel is used in Alaska (22.7 percent of state energy use as opposed to a 3.5 percent average nationally) (EIA 2008a). Table 3 also shows the power generated from fossil fuels that is assigned to the residential, commercial, and industrial sectors as reported by the EIA. In the EIA tables (EIA 2008a), total energy use is reported, and to prevent double accounting, fuel oil, natural gas, and coal used to generate electricity are assigned to the electrical sector. This material is converted to electricity and sold to the other sectors. The adjusted table accounts for all the energy consumed by those three sectors, including power generated by thermo mechanical systems (electricity generated by using fossil fuel).

One final comment about the EIA data: EIA energy values are derived from sales data and other sources. The survey methods for collecting estimates of wood consumed within the state are in part derived by combining Census Bureau and EIA survey information (EIA 2008d).

Additional Data

The Alaska Housing Manual (AHFC 2000) provides specific information relative to existing heating systems used in Alaska. This source reports that forced-air furnaces are very popular in the Anchorage-Valley area of Alaska, but fairly rare in other areas of the state. In other regions of Alaska, hydronic heating systems with baseboards or radiant floor systems are the standard. This source makes reference to space heaters produced by Toyo, Monitor, and Rinnai,[3] but provides no information relative to level of use.

In 2007, the FEDC completed a survey to assess community and consumer interest in use of pellet fuel (Robb 2007). Respondents were from the three major population areas of the state, including greater Fairbanks, central Alaska (Anchorage, Valley, and Kenai), and southeast Alaska. Survey questions were designed to collect information relative to current fuel types being used, current levels of energy use in both primary and secondary systems, fuel price, and the characteristics of existing wood-burning equipment. The updated Census Bureau household information can be used with FEDC survey data to obtain updated estimates of volumes of renewable wood energy being used for secondary heating in the various regions of Alaska.

---

[3] The use of trade or firm names in this publication is for reader information and does not imply endorsement by the U.S. Department of Agriculture of any product or service.

Table 3—Sources of energy consumed by various segments of the Alaska economy, 2005

Source	Alaska distribution	Residential sector	Commercial sector	Industrial sector	Transport sector[a]	Electric power	Total
	Percent				*Trillion Btu*		
Asphalt/roads	0.2	0	0	1.2	0	0	1.2
Aviation	.2	0	0	0	1.4	0	1.4
Biomass	.4	2.8	0.5	0.1	0	0	3.4
Coal	1.8	0.7	7.2	0	0	6.1	14.0
Distillate fuel	9.2	9.4	5.9	11.1	43.7	3.1	73.2
Ethanol	0	0	0	0	0.5	0	0.5
Hydroelectric	1.8	5.1	6.7	2.8	0	0	14.6
Jet fuel	22.7	0	0	0	181.1	0	181.1
Kerosene	0	.2	0	0	0	0	.2
Liquefied petroleum gas	.1	.8	.1	0	0	0	.9
Lubricants	.1	0	0	.1	.5	0	.6
Motor gas	4.5	0	.9	.5	34.3	0	35.7
Natural gas	54.3	18.1	16.9	356.7	2.7	39.5	433.9
Other	.0	.1	.1	0	0	0	.2
Other petroleum	4.3	0	0	34.3	0	0	34.3
Residual fuel	.6	0	0	0	.1	4.4	4.5
Total[b]	100	37.2	38.3	406.8	264.3	53.1	799.7
Fossil electricity consumed		1.9	2.5	1.10			
Total energy consumption		39.1	40.8	407.9			
Electricity sold to sector[c]		7.0 (34.8%)	9.2 (45.8%)	3.9 (19.4%)			20.1 (100%)

[a] Includes passenger vehicles.

[b] This total does not take into account transfers of electricity from the power sector to the other sectors. Thus, electricity from the power sector was added to the residential, commercial, and industrial sectors to account for all the energy consumed by those sectors.

[c] Electricity sold in Alaska is generated both by hydro sources and fossil fuel plants. The generation of electricity from fossil fuels is very inefficient. Fossil fuels consumed by the electric power sector are converted to electricity and sold to the other sectors. Minor amounts of electricity are utilized by the electric power sector and the amounts of energy leaving the generating plants are subject to transmission loss, prior to being sold to the various other sectors of the Alaska economy.

Btu = British thermal unit.

Note: The table contains rounding errors owing to the energy amounts in the source being in units of 1 trillion Btu.

Source: EIA 2008a: tables 7, 8, 9, 10, 11, and 12.

The FEDC survey represented information supplied by homeowners, a subset of total housing units. The reported usage of the major source of energy (fuel oil in Fairbanks and natural gas in Anchorage) for home heating was higher than those reported for all housing units in the Census Bureau housing survey. This trend in the data suggests that the source of heating energy for rental units may differ from that of owned units. The authors were unable to locate any data relative to rental units that would confirm this speculation.

Estimates of Current Use of RWEP for Home Heating in Alaska

Combining the data from the Census Bureau, EIA, and FEDC allows calculation of the volumes of wood currently being used for primary and secondary heating in Alaska census tracts. This was accomplished by using a three-stage process. First, Census Bureau 2000 data were updated by using 2006 Census QuickFacts (U.S. Census Bureau 2006b) data to reflect the number of housing units using distillate fuels (fuel oil, kerosene, and liquefied petroleum gas) for heating. The housing numbers were adjusted by removing all apartment units that were in buildings with five or more units. The housing units were also adjusted to reflect occupancy (half of unoccupied units were considered as unheated) and the smaller size of mobile homes (half of mobile homes were subtracted). This provided an adjusted estimate of the number of household units in each census track that were using distillate fuels.

Second, by using the EIA energy values (EIA 2008a) for residential use of distillate fuels and the adjusted number of housing units from step 1, average Btu usage for a unit was calculated. Given the temperature extremes that exist in the state, the authors were reluctant to apply this average to the census tracts without some weighting factor to account for the increased number of heating days and severity of winters in northern areas of the state.

The energy required to heat a house for a winter season is based on a combination of factors (e.g., quality of construction and insulation, size of the living area being heated, severity of the climate, fuel used, efficiency of the heating system), but a complete analysis of all of these factors was beyond the scope of this project. To simplify the analysis, it was assumed that all of these factors, other than climate, would be averaged. The impact of climate would be reflected by degree days using 65 °F as the basis (ACRC 2009).

Third, by using information from the Alaska Climate Research Center (ACRC 2009), the census tracts were assigned a reported degree-day value for a community within each census tract. Given that airports have a constant need for current weather information, an attempt was made to use airport locations whenever possible. If an airport location was not reported, a named community was used.

Given an estimate of the number of housing units and a weighting value to account for climate, the average house Btu value from step 2 was prorated to each census tract by using the number of housing units times number of degree days. The resulting estimates of annual Btu requirement for heating are presented in table 4. It shows the average for the state as almost 113 million Btu per home.

Table 4—Annual British thermal units (Btu) required for home heating in Alaska areas defined by Census Bureau tracts (derived from usage of distillate fuels)

Region	Borough/census area	Equivalent number of housing units	Btu per home
AA	Aleutians S. Borough	544	96,125,892
	Aleutians W. Borough	1,386	89,504,797
	Nome	2,786	136,762,610
	North Slope Borough	895	195,772,366
	Northwest Arctic Borough	1,825	155,655,733
	Wade Hampton Census Area	1,686	127,711,114
	Yukon-Koyukuk Census Area	2,135	146,074,149
	Total and average	11,257	137,140,799
GA	Anchorage	3,940	104,717,312
	Kenai Peninsula	10,213	111,828,488
	Matanuska-Susitna	9,080	106,087,539
	Valdez-Cordova	3,226	94,485,621
	Total and average	26,460	106,684,892
GF	Denali	806	131,081,671
	Fairbanks North Star	19,922	139,823,116
	Southeast Fairbanks	1,757	148,144,492
	Total and average	22,485	140,159,841
SE	Haines	873	86,394,283
	Juneau	7,083	85,754,177
	Ketchikan	4,072	71,561,831
	Prince of Wales-Outer Ketchikan	1,800	71,561,831
	Sitka	2,432	72,241,943
	Skagway-Hoonah-Angoon	1,515	86,444,291
	Wrangell-Petersburg	2,298	77,072,742
	Yakutat	347	92,395,275
	Total and average	20,421	79,278,059
SW	Bethel	4,180	127,711,114
	Bristol Bay	633	111,058,360
	Dillingham	1,749	114,078,860
	Kodiak Island	3,892	88,634,653
	Lake and Peninsula	1,029	111,058,360
	Total and average	11,483	109,980,779
State	Total and average	92,106	112,913,618

Note: AA = Aleutians and Arctic, GA = greater Anchorage, GF = greater Fairbanks, SE = southeast, and SW = southwest.

Estimated volumes of firewood consumed annually in Alaska were based on household Btu values derived from EIA, Census Bureau, and expanded FEDC data. The results for the major population centers in the state are reported in table 5. In the calculations, the Btu value assigned to the firewood assumed that the material had a moisture content of 50 percent and it was burned in a unit with a combustion efficiency of 60 percent. Using procedures outlined in Briggs (1994), such material would produce approximately 2,550 Btu/lb. The weight of the same material dried to 20 percent moisture content would be approximately 62 percent of green weight and have approximately a recoverable Btu value of 5,000 Btu/lb.

Table 5—Estimated volumes of firewood consumed annually in Alaska[a]

Region	Number of homes using wood as primary source of heat	Primary heat, firewood	Primary heat, green wood	Primary heat, green wood	Number of homes using wood as secondary source of heat	Secondary heat source volumes[b]	Total volume of primary and secondary usage
		Pounds	Tons	Cords		Cords	Cords
Aleutians and Arctic	1,337	75,541,179	37,771	15,108	2,612	5,225	20,333
Greater Anchorage	3,578	144,385,804	72,193	28,877	18,103	36,205	65,082
Greater Fairbanks	1,590	88,923,133	44,462	17,785	4,755	9,510	27,295
Southeast	1,698	52,098,096	26,049	10,420	3,894	7,787	18,207
Southwest	430	20,066,712	10,033	4,013	1,863	3,726	7,739
Total	8,632	381,014,924	190,507	76,203	31,227	62,453	138,656

[a] Based on household British thermal unit values derived from Energy Information Administration distillate fuels, Census Bureau housing data, and expanded Fairbanks Economic Development Corporation (FEDC) survey volumes. It was assumed that the firewood had a moisture content of 50 percent and it was burned in a unit with a combustion efficiency of 60 percent, producing about 2,550 Btu/lb.

[b] Based on FEDC pellet fuel survey, with a median value of two cords per owner-occupied housing unit. The Aleutians and Arctic, and Southwest census tracts were not included in the FEDC survey. The secondary use percentage from Greater Fairbanks was applied to the Aleutian and Arctic region and the Southeast rate to the Southwest region to obtain the estimates above. No estimate for secondary firewood use in rental units is included.

Note: All green weights have been converted to cords based on a factor of 2.5 tons per cord. Use of this factor will underestimate softwood volumes and overestimate hardwood volumes.

Sources: EIA 2008a; Robb 2007; U.S. Census Bureau 2000, 2006b.

An estimated 8,632 homes in Alaska use wood as their primary source of heat. The total volume of firewood used annually for heating is 76,203 cords.

Given the above procedures and conversion factors, it is estimated that there are 8,632 homes using wood as the primary source of heat in Alaska (table 5). The total volume of firewood used annually as the primary source of heating is 76,203 cords. Given the FEDC survey, it was also possible to estimate the number of homes (31,227 units) and volume of firewood (53,502 cords) used in secondary heating. In total, it is estimated that about 138,656 cords of wood are used as a primary and secondary source of heat in Alaska. It might be assumed that the firewood removals from the Alaska forests are equal to the same number. This, however, is not necessarily the case. The relationship between volume used and harvest is discussed later in this report.

Cost Comparison for Alternative Energy Sources

From the consumer's point of view, any economic assessment of fuels and sources of energy must provide an answer to the basic question, "What will each alternative cost?" There are two components of cost. First is the cost of purchasing equipment (fixed costs) for a specific fuel option and second is the cost for annual maintenance and the fuel itself (variable). Although the question seems simple, the process of developing the answer, given the maze of measurement units used in the commerce of fossil and renewable forms of energy, is complex.

Given the hydroscopic nature of wood, an understanding of moisture content and its impact on recoverable energy is critical to this report. It must be recognized that all fuels (e.g., coal, gas, oil, and wood) may include moisture that must be removed in the combustion process. In gas and oil, the moisture content is most commonly minimal and the efficiency of the burning equipment itself results in a loss of energy available for heating or powering a process. The most logical way to compare cost of alternative sources of energy is to compare the cost of the Btu recoverable from each product. In this project, the recoverable Btu value of selected alternative sources of energy were calculated to show the break-even price that could be paid for the alternative.

The commerce of wood and the units of measurements therein are poorly understood by the general public. Many individuals in the forest products industry are just becoming exposed to the conversion factors and evaluation of biomass-related energy products. In many areas, costs for purchasing standing trees, harvesting, and delivery to mills is readily available. In such locations, mills procuring wood advertise prices they are willing to pay for specific species and products. In many heavily forested states, information relative to standing timber and delivered values of forest products are collected and published by university extension agencies and state-supported marketing programs. Such is not the case in Alaska. Another complication associated with Alaska is that almost all of the timber harvest in the region processed by sawmills is of high quality and large size. The mills produce residual products (chips, sawdust, bark, or mixtures thereof) that can be used as a source of energy, but Alaska lacks mills that process timber directly from the round-log form to fiber. Given these Alaska-related problems, the following is a review of timber economics in general. It has been assumed that harvesting for energy products would require low-quality logs. Generally available information from Oregon (ODF 2009), an area whose conditions and timber species are somewhat comparable to those of southeast Alaska, has been used to develop a hypothetical minimum price for low-grade logs and young growth harvested in Alaska.

An explanation of selling prices of wood can best be reviewed by commonly relating them to the following two situations. In the first case, a landowner that owns standing timber may sell the material to a logger or mill as standing timber. In this instance, the value of the wood is referred to as "stumpage value." The logger or the mill owner has the right to enter onto the land, harvest the timber, and deliver it to the mill. The logger pays the landowner for the value of timber harvested, or "stumpage." The costs of harvesting and transportation to the mill are not included in the "stumpage value." In Alaska, stumpage may be purchased from the U.S. Forest Service, several state agencies, Native landowners, and occasionally in small volumes from private landowners.

Moving along the chain of commerce to the mill owner that produces products from logs, the cost of the material delivered to the mill includes the stumpage value, all in-woods harvesting costs, cost of trucking or transportation to the mill, and any overhead costs for management, supervision, and scaling of material. The delivered cost is synonymous with the term "pond value."[4] An excellent explanation of various log values is available at the Oregon Department of Forestry (ODF) Web site http://www.oregon.gov/ODF.

It is certain that costs and prices in Alaska will be higher than anything reported from the ODF (2009) site. But as an example, the average pond price for low-grade logs in the fourth quarter of 2008 from this source (ODF 2009) is reviewed. The average price for 46 sales of low-grade western hemlock and spruce (*Picea* spp.) logs was calculated as $271 per thousand board feet (mbf). A review of selected sales from state lands for the same period indicated a woods-run stumpage price for all grades of spruce logs of approximately $100/mbf and slightly less than $50/mbf for hemlock. As stated, this is an average price for all harvested grades. The prorated stumpage value for low-grade logs could be 25 to 50 percent of the average values. If these prices are applied to the pond price, dollar amounts paid by the mill owner would be distributed in the following manner, assuming the end product was low-grade hemlock. Approximately $25/mbf would be paid to the landowner to cover the cost of the wood. An amount of $232.50/mbf would be paid to the contractor delivering the logs to cover harvesting, trucking, in-woods supervision, and hopefully some amount for profit and risk. A small amount, estimated at approximately 5 percent for the purposes of this example or $13.50/mbf, would go to cover the cost of scaling and yard handling.

---

[4] The term "pond value" is a holdover from the days when logs were stored in water once delivered to the mill. Water-stored logs were protected against log-boring insects and, in the days before mechanized equipment, easy to move from storage by floating them to the mill.

Firewood is traditionally sold by the cord and the final question that must be addressed is, "Given a pond price of $271/mbf, what would be the value per cord?" First, the material purchased at the stated rates is low grade and tends to be in logs with small scaling diameters (less than 12-in diameter) and the ratio of cords to thousand board feet in such material is high. The ratio is also extremely sensitive to the length of the scaled logs. Based on experience and data from two young-growth projects conducted by the Alaska Wood Utilization Center[5] (Brackley et al. 2009b, Nicholls and Brackley 2009), the conversion factor could range from 2.5 to 4.5 cords/mbf of scaled material. The cord price for this range would be between $108.40 and $60.22 per cord of unprocessed wood (not cut to length or split).

Table 6 presents information relative to the dollar value of a therm of energy (a therm is defined as 100,000 Btu of energy) from various alternative fuels. In table 7, the value of selected RWEP (green cords, dry cords, tons of green material, tons of dry material, and tons of pellets) is shown based on the dollars per therm from alternative sources. The tables have been prepared so the reader can reference the costs of the alternatives in terms of the commonly utilized units of measurement. To interpret the tables, using fuel oil as an example, if the price per gallon is $4.00,

---

[5] Nicholls, D.; Brackley, A.M. 2008. House log drying rates in southeast Alaska for covered and uncovered softwood logs. Unpublished data. On file with: USDA Forest Service, Pacific Northwest Research Station, Alaska Wood Utilization Research and Development Center, 204 Siginaka Way, Sitka, AK 99835.

Table 6—Value of selected energy alternatives based on assigned value (dollars) per therm of energy

Energy alternative (unit)	Assigned value of 1 therm of energy[a]										
	$2.00	$2.25	$2.50	$2.75	$3.00	$3.25	$3.50	$3.75	$4.00	$5.00	$6.00
	Dollars per unit										
Fuel oil (gallon)	2.77	3.12	3.47	3.81	4.16	4.51	4.85	5.20	5.55	6.93	8.32
Propane (gallon)	1.72	1.94	2.15	2.37	2.59	2.80	3.02	3.23	3.45	4.31	5.17
Natural gas (Mcf)	20.60	23.18	25.75	28.33	30.90	33.48	36.05	38.63	41.20	51.50	61.80
Electricity (kW)	0.07	0.08	0.09	0.09	0.10	0.11	0.12	0.13	0.14	0.17	0.20
Wood pellets (ton)	340	383	425	468	510	553	595	638	680	850	1,020
Wood 50%MC (cord)	425	478	531	584	638	691	744	797	850	1,063	1,275
Wood 20%MC (cord)	425	478	531	584	638	691	744	797	850	1,063	1,275
Wood 50%MC (ton)	170	191	213	234	255	276	298	319	340	425	510
Wood 20%MC (ton)	272	306	340	374	408	442	476	510	544	680	816

[a] A therm of energy equals 100,000 British thermal units (Btu). Given the assigned value per therm, each row presents the dollar value of an alternative fuel in terms of the units commonly used in commerce as the basis for selling and purchasing the energy product. The values in each column represent the maximum price that a consumer can pay for the alternative. If the market price for an alternative is lower than the listed value, there is an economic incentive for the consumer to change to that energy source. When considering changes in energy source, the consumer must also take into consideration the cost (investment) for equipment upgrades and the conversion efficiency of the alternative.

Note: All references to moisture content (MC) are green basis. The recoverable Btu from a volume of wood is constant over a range of moisture contents. As a volume of wood dries, the weight of the material decreases but the gross heating value (GHV) of the material increases. Weight × GHV = a constant value.

Table 7—Dollar value of British thermal units (Btu) in selected renewable wood energy products based on Btu value of alternative sources of energy

Wood fuel and burning equipment characteristic				Alternative source of energy to be replaced			You can pay up to:
Unit of commerce	Moisture content	Burning unit efficiency	Recoverable energy	Cost	Heating unit efficiency	Adjusted cost for recoverable energy	Cost per unit to replace alternative
	- - - Percent - - -		Therm[a]	Dollars per therm	Percent	- - - - - - Dollars - - - - - -	
Fuel oil at $2.00 per gallon:							
Green cord	50	50	106.3	1.44	85	1.70	180
Dry cord	20	50	106.3	1.44	85	1.70	180
Green ton	50	80	68.0	1.44	85	1.70	115
Dry ton	20	50	68.0	1.44	85	1.70	115
Dry ton	20	80	108.8	1.44	85	1.70	185
Pellets ton	6.5	80	127.2	1.44	85	1.70	216
Fuel oil at $4.00 per gallon:							
Green cord	50	50	106.3	2.88	85	3.39	361
Dry cord	20	50	106.3	2.88	85	3.39	361
Green ton	50	80	68.0	2.88	85	3.39	231
Dry ton	20	50	68.0	2.88	85	3.39	231
Dry ton	20	80	108.8	2.88	85	3.39	369
Pellets ton	6.5	80	127.2	2.88	85	3.39	432
Natural gas at $10 per thousand cubic feet:							
Green cord	50	50	106.3	0.97	90	1.08	115
Dry cord	20	50	106.3	0.97	90	1.08	115
Green ton	50	80	68.0	0.97	90	1.08	73
Dry ton	20	50	68.0	0.97	90	1.08	73
Dry ton	20	80	108.8	0.97	90	1.08	118
Pellets ton	6.5	80	127.2	0.97	90	1.08	137
Natural gas at $15 per thousand cubic feet:							
Green cord	50	50	106.3	1.46	90	1.62	172
Dry cord	20	50	106.3	1.46	90	1.62	172
Green ton	50	80	68.0	1.46	90	1.62	110
Dry ton	20	50	68.0	1.46	90	1.62	110
Dry ton	20	80	108.8	1.46	90	1.62	176
Pellets ton	6.5	80	127.2	1.46	90	1.62	206
Electricity at $0.10 per kilowatthour:							
Green cord	50	50	106.3	2.93	90	3.26	346
Dry cord	20	50	106.3	2.93	90	3.26	346
Green ton	50	80	170.0	2.93	90	3.26	554
Dry ton	20	50	68.0	2.93	90	3.26	221
Dry ton	20	80	108.8	2.93	90	3.26	354
Pellets ton	6.5	80	127.2	2.93	90	3.26	414
Electricity at $0.15 per kilowatthour:							
Green cord	50	50	106.3	4.40	90	4.88	519
Dry cord	20	50	106.3	4.40	90	4.88	519
Green ton	50	80	170.0	4.40	90	4.88	830
Dry ton	20	50	68.0	4.40	90	4.88	332
Dry ton	20	80	108.8	4.40	90	4.88	531
Pellets ton	6.5	80	127.2	4.40	90	4.88	621

[a] A therm is a term used to describe 100,000 British thermal units of energy.

then the value per therm (100,000 Btu) is $2.88 (see table 7). If the fuel were burned in a unit that was 85 percent efficient, the cost per therm would be adjusted to $3.39. The value of a cord of wood at 50 percent moisture content, burned in a stove with 50 percent efficiency, would provide 106.3 therms of energy. Based on the cost of $3.39 per Btu for oil, a person could pay up to $361 for a cord of wood to replace oil at $4.00/gal (see table 7). Interpretation of the data at this point will depend on the self-motivation of the individual user and their willingness to invest in equipment and cut, transport, and split wood. A willing user that has a source of wood on the stump can reduce energy cost to a fraction of the above amounts.

Given the above analysis, a landowner or logger in the business of selling firewood can charge up to the stated amount of the alternative for cut-to-length and split material and be competitive with the alternative. If they can reduce their price to less than the above amount and are satisfied with the profit margin, they have a competitive advantage over the alternative at the stated price. The lower the price, the more competitive they become and the more incentive the user has to make an investment in new heating equipment (capital costs required to replace fuel systems with RWEP could be very high) to convert from the alternative to RWEP. If the cost of delivering the material to a wood processing yard is $108.40, the high end of the estimated delivered cost, there is still a tremendous opportunity ($252.60 obtained by subtracting the $108.40 per cord price for delivery to the wood yard from $361 alternative cost of oil) to make a profit from the activity.

Potential Demand for RWEP for Home Heating in Alaska

Given this analysis, it is concluded that at $3.00/gal for fuel oil there is a price incentive for users of distillate fuels to convert to RWEP. With recent electricity prices over $0.10/kWh, there is also a price incentive for consumers using this form of energy to convert. For the purposes of this report, it is assumed that the maximum potential is in fact best defined as the Btu level used by consumers using distillate fuels. Estimates of the maximum potential volumes of RWEP that might be required annually to meet this level of demand are shown in table 8.

In table 8, the 2006 updated Census Bureau data have been adjusted so that the number of housing units more closely corresponds to the EIA-defined residential sector. The adjustments are the same as reviewed previously in the report. Data for EIA residential distillate fuel use was then prorated to the number of housing units, weighted by the number of degree days for a named location in the census tract. Once the census tract distillate Btu value was available, it was converted to an equivalent Btu of RWEP assuming that the wood was dried to 20 percent moisture content and burned at a combustion efficiency of 60 percent. Any stimulus

At $3.00/gal for fuel oil, there is a price incentive for users of distillate fuels to convert to renewable wood energy products.

Table 8—Annual volume of wood or pellets required to replace distillate fuel used in residential and commercial sectors in Alaska census tracts

Borough/census area	Adjusted number of housing units	Total distillate use	Green wood[a]	Green wood[b]	Wood pellets[c]	Pellet raw material if used for drying[d]	Green wood[e]	Pellet raw material if used for drying[d]
		Therms[f]	*Tons*	*Cords*	*Tons*	- - - - - - - - - Cords - - - - - - - - -		
Aleutians S. Borough	544	523,069	10,256	4,103	4,387	5,331	6,687	8,689
Aleutians W. Borough	1,386	1,240,670	24,327	9,731	10,407	12,644	15,861	20,610
Nome	2,786	3,809,589	74,698	29,879	31,954	38,824	48,703	63,284
North Slope Borough	895	1,751,248	34,338	13,735	14,689	17,847	22,389	29,091
Northwest Arctic Borough	1,825	2,840,027	55,687	22,275	23,822	28,943	36,308	47,178
Wade Hampton Census Area	1,686	2,153,769	42,231	16,892	18,065	21,950	27,534	35,778
Yukon-Koyukuk Census Area	2,135	3,119,137	61,160	24,464	26,163	31,788	39,876	51,814
Total	11,257	15,437,508	302,696	121,078	129,488	157,327	197,358	256,444
Anchorage	3,940	4,126,350	80,909	32,364	34,611	42,053	52,753	68,546
Kenai Peninsula	10,213	11,421,265	223,946	89,579	95,800	116,397	146,013	189,727
Matanuska-Susitna	9,080	9,632,864	188,880	75,552	80,799	98,171	123,150	160,019
Valdez-Cordova	3,226	3,048,145	59,768	23,907	25,567	31,064	38,968	50,635
Total	26,460	28,228,624	553,502	221,401	236,778	287,685	360,884	468,926
Denali	806	1,056,854	20,723	8,289	8,865	10,771	13,511	17,556
Fairbanks North Star	19,922	27,855,719	546,191	218,476	233,650	283,884	356,116	462,732
Southeast Fairbanks	1,757	2,602,632	51,032	20,413	21,830	26,524	33,273	43,234
Total	22,485	31,515,204	617,945	247,178	264,345	321,179	402,900	523,522
Haines	873	754,220	14,789	5,915	6,326	7,686	9,642	12,529
Juneau	7,083	6,074,363	119,105	47,642	50,951	61,905	77,657	100,906
Ketchikan	4,072	2,914,291	57,143	22,857	24,445	29,700	37,257	48,411
Prince Wales–Outer Ketchikan	1,800	1,288,390	25,263	10,105	10,807	13,130	16,471	21,402
Sitka	2,432	1,756,925	34,450	13,780	14,737	17,905	22,461	29,186
Skagway-Hoonah-Angoon	1,515	1,309,491	25,676	10,271	10,984	13,345	16,741	21,753
Wrangell-Petersburg	2,298	1,770,807	34,722	13,889	14,853	18,047	22,639	29,416
Yakutat	347	320,715	6,289	2,515	2,690	3,268	4,100	5,328
Total	20,421	16,189,201	317,435	126,974	135,793	164,988	206,968	268,931
Bethel	4,180	5,338,865	104,684	41,873	44,782	54,410	68,254	88,688
Bristol Bay	633	703,116	13,787	5,515	5,898	7,166	8,989	11,680
Dillingham	1,749	1,995,090	39,119	15,648	16,735	20,332	25,506	33,142
Kodiak Island	3,892	3,449,628	67,640	27,056	28,935	35,156	44,101	57,304
Lake and Peninsula	1,029	1,142,763	22,407	8,963	9,585	11,646	14,609	18,983
Total	11,483	12,629,462	247,637	99,055	105,934	128,710	161,459	209,797
Total all	92,106	104,000,000	2,039,216	815,686	872,337	1,059,889	1,329,569	1,727,620

[a] At a combustion efficiency of 60 percent.
[b] At 2.5 tons per cord.
[c] At a moisture content of 6.5 percent and a combustion efficiency of 75 percent.
[d] When part of the raw material is used as an energy source for drying, raw material requirement is increased by up to 25 percent.
[e] Calculated by multiplying the residential amount by 1.63 (multiplier is ratio of commercial oil use in relation to residential oil use; from EIA data (EIA 2008a)).
[f] A therm is a term used to describe 100,000 British thermal units of energy.

that would increase the combustion efficiency of the burning units will reduce the required replacement volumes. British thermal unit equivalent of wood pellets was based on a moisture content of 6.5 percent and a combustion efficiency of 75 percent. This efficiency is slightly less than levels quoted by pellet stove vendors and, again, a higher level of efficiency would result in a decrease in the replacement volume.

Given the above adjustments, it was estimated that the maximum potential annual demand for RWEP to replace distillate fuels for heating in the residential sector of Alaska is about 815,000 cords of green wood or about 872,000 tons of wood pellets (see table 8). If all of the liquid fuels used by the residential and commercial sectors in Alaska were converted to solid wood energy, it is estimated that 1.3 million cords of green wood would be required annually. With respect to wood pellets, a portion of the raw material delivered to the mill is often burned and used to dry the remaining material. Use of part of the raw material as an energy source for drying will increase raw material requirements up to 25 percent. The seventh and ninth columns in table 8 provide an estimate of the volume of material that would be required to produce pellets including material used for drying. The estimated volume of wood that would satisfy the potential demand for wood pellets is about 1.06 million cords of material for the residential sector and about 1.73 million cords of material for both the residential and commercial sectors. This level of RWEP use would represent less than 40 percent of the highest harvest level reported by the Alaska timber industry (Brackley et al. 2009a).

Although table 8 provides potential demand in terms of firewood and pellets, in reality, a portion of the market will be captured by each product. In this report, the demand is based on replaceable fossil fuel Btu. As each product (firewood, pellets, compressed logs, chips, etc.) enters the market, the remaining volume required from other entries is based on the remaining required Btu. In the future, liquid fossil fuel may also be replaced by liquid bio products.

Discussion

Replacement Based on Economics

The conversion among the various sources of energy, especially RWEP, is complex and price itself may not be the limiting factor. Natural gas and electric heating systems are compact and can be used in almost any building. Systems that use fuel oil and other petroleum-base products require tanks, but the space required for tanks is minor. In some areas of extreme cold, these tanks must be located in a partially heated area. On the other hand, renewable wood energy products require

The conversion among various sources of energy, especially renewable wood energy products, is complex, and price itself may not be the limiting factor.

A year's supply of firewood (assuming up to 8 cords) will require up to 1,100 ft³ of space (i.e., a building with a floor area of 14 by 14 ft if the wood is piled 6 ft high).

considerable storage areas and handling. A year's supply of firewood (assuming up to 8 cords) will require up to 1,100 ft³ of space (i.e., a building with a floor area of 14 by 14 ft if the wood is piled 6 ft high). Ideally, this storage area should be covered but of sufficient size to allow ventilation to promote drying. In most coastal areas of Alaska, the lowest moisture content resulting from air drying will be 15 to 16 percent green basis. Slightly lower moisture contents may be attained in inland areas such as Fairbanks.

One year's supply of wood pellets (6 tons) would require floor area of approximately 100 ft² stacked to delivered pallet height. During the heating season, the user must be willing to frequently move fuel from storage to the area where it will be used. Much of the extra work associated with RWEP can be minimized when constructing new homes, designed from the start to utilize these sources of energy, and assuming the evolution of an industry to efficiently deliver the product. Many existing homes, especially in areas of higher population density, were designed for use with fossil fuels or electricity, and this may restrict conversion opportunities.

Table 7 identifies some of the realities when considering replacement of fossil energy sources with RWEP in Alaska. First, given the price for natural gas in the Anchorage-Valley area, there is little price incentive to convert from this source of energy. Natural gas is one of the cleaner burning nonrenewable fossil fuels and in any system to tax carbon, will receive the most favorable treatment of any of the fossil fuels.

The lowest cost for electricity in the populated areas of the state is approximately $0.10/kWh. Electricity produced by hydro, wind, and solar sources is a very clean form of energy. Electricity produced from fossil fuels, however, is a totally different situation. In general, the Btu input of liquid fossil fuel to produce electricity is roughly three times the energy of the resulting electricity. The impact of this is felt in small rural communities where electricity has traditionally been supplied by diesel-powered generators. In such communities, it is not uncommon to find electricity prices of $0.30/kWh or more (AEA 2008). According to EIA (2008c) data, 18 percent of the energy used by the residential sector in Alaska is from electricity. Available census data (U.S. Census Bureau 2006b) indicate that only 10 percent of the Alaska housing units are heated with electricity. Even at the lowest prices for this source of energy, there is an economic incentive to convert to various RWEPs if the housing can be modified to provide fuel storage.

In general, the Btu input of liquid fossil fuel to produce electricity is roughly three times the energy of the resulting electricity.

Twenty-seven percent of the energy used by the residential sector in Alaska is in the distillate fuels (fuel oil and liquefied petroleum) (see fig. 3). Thirty-eight percent of the housing units are heated with these fuels (see fig. 2). Based on table 7, at a fuel oil price of $2.00/gal the economic incentive to convert to RWEP is minimal, unless the user has a source of standing timber or material that can be converted to firewood using "sweat equity." At a price of $2.00/gal there is little opportunity for a fuel dealer to make a profit from RWEP sales. Although not listed in table 7, the interpolated value of a cord of green wood at $3.00/gal of fuel oil is $270. At this price, the users of "sweat equity" and fuel dealers are both enabled. At prices above $3.00/gal, there is an obvious economic incentive for homeowners to convert, as the cost saving for RWEP is sufficient to cover the capital costs for converting oil burning equipment to RWEP equipment.

Energy Sources Most Likely To Be Replaced by RWEP

As stated in the "Introduction," replacement of traditional sources of energy for home heating and conversion to RWEP will be a function of a number of factors. The ultimate objectives of this project are to determine initial estimates of the potential volumes that are candidates for replacement and provide an introduction to some of the factors that will impact the rate of replacement and the ultimate amount of replacement.

In addition to identification of factors, there are many questions relative to how the factors will interact to promulgate change. It is certain that conversion to RWEP will take place over a period of years. The Alaska Housing Manual (AHFC 2000) reported that the most common heating system used in the Anchorage-Valley region were centralized, gas fired, hot air systems. In other areas of the state, centralized oil fired hydronic systems are the norm. In new home construction or in upgrades of heating systems, it is possible to integrate fossil fuels and RWEP into a common air or water distribution system. Burners that incorporate oil, solid wood, or pellets in one integrated unit or as two independent units are available. There would be more incentive to install multifuel systems where high-priced sources of energy are used. In the long term, transparent (i.e., requiring relatively minor changes to burner system and fuel delivery method) conversion to liquid RWEP is an option for homeowners with fuel-oil based systems. It is more likely, however, that most of the initial conversion to RWEP will involve increased use of space heaters and fireplace inserts, thus reducing the dependence on the high-cost energy alternatives.

Sources of Renewable Wood Energy Material

Some individuals may assume that conversion and utilization of RWEP in accordance with the previously stated numbers will result in a cord-for-cord increase in the harvest levels from the forests of the state. For many reasons, however, this is not the case. A complete analysis and statement of the reasons why the assumption is incorrect is beyond the scope of this paper, but a few comments are appropriate.

The ultimate objectives of this project are to determine initial estimates of the potential volumes that are candidates for replacement and provide an introduction to some of the factors that will impact the rate of replacement and the ultimate amount of replacement.

First, the U.S. Department of Agriculture, Forest Service, Forest Inventory and Analysis (FIA) Program is charged by Congress with maintaining an inventory of timber volumes in the forest (public and private) of the United States. Trees defined as timber include stems that can currently be harvested into saw logs, those that have the potential to grow into logs at some future date, and trees that owing to poor form (i.e., they are crooked) or rot, cannot produce a saw log. By definition, growth takes place only on the growing-stock trees—those that currently are suitable for producing saw logs or have the potential to grow into saw logs. Given these definitions, if a tree that does not include a saw log or have the potential to grow into a saw log is removed from the woods and used, the removal has no impact on growth as defined by the FIA. In the past, timber volumes have been defined in terms of merchantability standards. The standards of the past excluded material in tops and limbs left in the woods from the inventoried timber volumes. Tops, limbs, rough and rotten trees, and trees below standards of merchantability, however, can all be harvested for fiber and converted into energy products.

Also, residual products such as slabs, edgings, or sawdust from saw logs can be converted into energy products and the use of residuals does not result in any increase in the number of trees cut and harvested. The size of a residual-based industry, however, is somewhat limited by the capacity of the mills to process the solid wood product, such as lumber.

Many homeowners produce firewood from trees that do not grow in the forest or from dead and low-grade trees that are not considered as forest growing stock. Homeowners can also go into areas that have been logged and cut firewood from branches and tops that are left in the woods as slash. Use of these materials does not have any impact on growth.

If high-quality trees of saw-log quality or trees that have the potential to grow into saw-log-quality trees are harvested and used for energy products, there will be a reduction in growing stock material.

These are a few of the situations that need to be taken into account to determine the impact of energy use on the forest. As a rule of thumb, if high-quality trees of saw-log quality or trees that have the potential to grow into saw-log-quality trees are harvested and used for energy products, there will be a reduction in growing stock material. If, however, the material is from any other source (e.g., land not considered part of the forest, trees not of growing-stock quality, or parts of trees already harvested), it is in fact considered an increase in utilization of harvested material that has no impact as far as timber sustainability is concerned. Such changes in utilization may, however, have an impact on the sustainability of forest ecosystems when the concepts of biodiversity and related value of course woody debris are considered. A complete review of these issues is beyond the scope of this project.

Conclusions

The level and satisfaction of future demand for RWEP in Alaska really has little to do with the existence of a biomass resource. It is limited, however, by the size of the existing forest products industry, the industry's capacity to economically harvest wood, and society's willingness to convert. In addition, conversion to RWEP will be a function of a national energy policy and price for alternatives. Lacking a national energy policy, a return to high market prices for oil will stimulate production of energy products and result in conversion. It is also possible that conversion will in part promote the development of a more vibrant forest products economy in Alaska.

Total conversion of oil and other liquid fuels used by the Alaska residential and commercial sectors to solid RWEPs would require in excess of 1.3 million cord equivalents of material annually. Although that volume may appear great to many people, in reality it represents the amount of wood required to supply raw material to one large pulp mill.

The economic incentive to convert to solid wood fuel exists at any heating oil price in excess of $3.00/gal. At this level, fixed costs are recovered in relatively short periods (5 years or less). A national energy policy may impact conversion by placing a tax on fossil fuels or providing tax credits to help cover the costs of converting to systems that use RWEPs (biomass).

Total conversion of oil and other liquid fuels used by the Alaska residential and commercial sectors to solid renewable wood energy products would require in excess of 1.3 million cord equivalents of material annually.

Acknowledgments

This report is based upon work supported by the University of Alaska and Cooperative State Research, Education and Extension Service, U.S. Department of Agriculture, under Agreement No. 2006-34158-17722. Any opinions, findings, conclusions, or recommendations expressed in this publication are those of the author(s) and do not necessarily reflect the view of the U.S. Department of Agriculture. Funds to support the Fairbanks Economic Development Corporation, Wood Pellet Market Survey activity were provided in part by USDA Forest Service Joint Venture Agreement PNW-07-JV-11261935-042 between the U.S. Forest Service, Pacific Northwest Forest Research Station, Alaska Wood Utilization Center, and the Fairbanks Economic Development Corporation.

Metric Equivalents

When you know:	Multiply by:	To find:
British thermal units (Btu)	1,050	Joules
Inches (in)	2.54	Centimeters
Feet (ft)	.305	Meters
Cubic feet (ft^3)	.0283	Cubic meters
Miles (mi)	1.609	Kilometers
Gallons (gal)	3.78	Liters
Thousand board feet, log scale (mbf)	4.5	Cubic meters, logs
Tons (ton)	907	Kilograms
Pounds (lb)	454	Grams
Degrees Fahrenheit	.56(°F − 32)	Degrees Celsius
British thermal units	3,412.14	Kilowatt-hour (kWh)

Common and Scientific Names

Common name	Scientific name
Alaska yellow-cedar	*Chamaecyparis nootkatensis* (D. Don) Spach
Black cottonwood	*Populus balsamifera* L. ssp. *trichocarpa* (Torr. & A. Gray ex Hook.) Brayshaw
Paper birch	*Betula papyrifera* Marsh.
Quaking aspen	*Populus tremuloides* Michx.
Red alder	*Alnus rubra* Bong.
Sitka spruce	*Picea sitchensis* (Bong.) Carriere
Western hemlock	*Tsuga heterophylla* (Raf.) Sarg.
Western redcedar	*Thuja plicata* Donn ex D. Don
White spruce	*Picea glauca* (Moench) Voss

Literature Cited

Alaska Climatic Research Center [ACRC]. 2009. Mean annual heating degree days for selected bases (1971–2000). http://climate.gi.alaska.edu/Climate/ Normals/HDD.html. (March 17, 2009).

Alaska Energy Authority [AEA]. 2008. Statistical report of the power cost equalization program, fiscal year 2007. 19th ed. February 2008. Juneau, AK: State of Alaska. 22 p.

Alaska Housing Finance Corporation [AHFC]. 2000. Alaska housing manual. 4th ed. Anchorage, AK: Research and Rural Development Division. 119 p. http://www.ahfc.state.ak.us/reference/housing_manual.cfm. (April 6, 2009).

Bowyer, J.L.; Shmulsky, R.; Haygreen, J.G. 2003. Forest products and wood science—an introduction. 4th ed. Ames, IA: Iowa State University Press. 554 p.

Brackley, A.M.; Haynes, R.W.; Alexander, S.J. 2009a. Timber harvests in Alaska: 1910–2006. Res. Note PNW-RN-560. Portland, OR: U.S. Department of Agriculture, Forest Service, Pacific Northwest Research Station. 24 p.

Brackley, A.M.; Nicholls, D.L.; Hannan, M. 2009b. An evaluation of the grades and value of red alder lumber in southeast Alaska. Gen. Tech. Rep. PNW-GTR-774. Portland, OR: U.S. Department of Agriculture, Forest Service, Pacific Northwest Research Station. 27 p.

Briggs, D. 1994. Forest products measurements and conversion factors: with special emphasis on the U.S. Pacific Northwest. IFR Contribution No. 75. Seattle, WA: University of Washington, College of Forest Resources. 168 p.

Bruce, D.; Schumacher, F.X. 1950. Forest mensuration. 3rd ed. New York: McGraw-Hill Book Company, Inc. 483 p.

Dunster, J.; Dunster, K. 1996. Dictionary of natural resource management. Vancouver, BC: UBC Press. 363 p.

Electronic Code of Federal Regulations [ECFR]. 2009. Title 40: protection of environment. Part 60—standards of performance for new stationary sources. http://ecfr.gpoaccess.gov/cgi/t/text/text-idx?c=ecfr;sid=c3e6eb575293d0041e7a768 e297b67d9;rgn=div6;view=text;node=40%3A6.0.1.1.1.65;idno=40;cc=ecfr. (June 16, 2009).

Energy Information Administration [EIA]. 2008a. Alaska—state energy data system (SEDS): production, 1960–2006. http://www.eia.doe.gov/emeu/states/ state.html?q_state_a=ak&q_state=ALASKA. (September 3, 2008). On file with: Allen Brackley, Pacific Northwest Research Station, Alaska Wood Utilization Research and Development Center, 204 Siginaka Way, Sitka, AK 99835.

Energy Information Administration [EIA]. 2008b. Consumption, price, and expenditure estimates—state energy data system. http://www.eia.doe.gov/emeu/ states/_seds.html. (November 2008).

Energy Information Administration [EIA]. 2008c. State energy profiles— Alaska. http://tonto.eia.doe.gov/state/state_energy_profiles.cfm?sid=AK. (September 3, 2008).

Energy Information Administration [EIA]. 2008d. Technical notes and documentation—state energy data system (SEDS). http://www.eia.doe.gov/ emeu/states/_seds_tech_notes.html. (September 3, 2008).

Eshleman, C. 2008. Fairbanks Borough mayor pushes for wood stove trade-in plan. Fairbanks Daily News-Miner. December 8. http://www.newsminer.com/ news/2008/dec/08/fairbanks-borough-mayor-jim-whitaker-pushes-wood-s/. (April 8, 2009).

Evans, D.S., ed. 2000. Terms of the trade. 4th ed. Eugene, OR: Random Length Publications, Inc. 425 p.

Husch, B.; Miller, C.I.; Beers, T.W. 1982. Forest mensuration. 3rd ed. New York: John Wiley & Sons. 402 p.

Ince, P.J. 1979. How to estimate the recoverable heat energy in wood and bark fuels. Gen. Tech. Rep. FPL-29. Madison, WI: U.S. Department of Agriculture, Forest Service, Forest Products Laboratory. 6 p.

Kollmann, F.F.P.; Cote, W.A. 1968. Principles of wood science and technology. Part 1 Solid wood. New York: Springer-Verlag. 592 p.

National Appliance Energy Conservation Act of 1987 [NAECA]. 42 U.S.C. Pub. L. 100-12; 101 Stat. 103.

Nicholls, D.; Brackley, A. 2009. House log drying rates in southeast Alaska for covered and uncovered softwood logs. Gen. Tech. Rep. PNW-GTR-782. Portland, OR: U.S. Department of Agriculture, Forest Service, Pacific Northwest Research Station. 18 p.

Nicholls, D.; Monserud, R.A.; Dykstra, D.P. 2009. International bioenergy synthesis—lessons learned and opportunities for the Western United States. Forest Ecology and Management. 257(8): 1647–1655.

Oregon Department of Forestry [ODF]. 2009. Log price information. http://www.oregon.gov/ODF/STATE_FORESTS/TIMBER_SALES/logpage. shtml. (April 9, 2009).

Patton-Mallory, M., ed. 2008. Woody biomass utilization strategy. FS-899. Washington, DC: U.S. Department of Agriculture, Forest Service. 17 p.

Robb, S. 2007. Survey to assess community support for pellet fuel—a report prepared for the Fairbanks Economic Development Corporation. Anchorage, AK: Information Insights, Inc. 36 p.

U.S. Census Bureau. 2000. American FactFinder, DP-4. profile of selected housing characteristics: 2000. http://factfinder.census.gov/servlet/QTTable?_bm=n&_lang=en&qr_name=DEC_2000_SF3_U_DP4&ds_name=DEC_2000_SF3_U&geo_id=04000US02. (July 1, 2008).

U.S. Census Bureau. 2004. Housing data between the censuses: the American housing survey. Census Rep. AHS/R/04-2. Washington, DC. 23 p.

U.S. Census Bureau. 2005a. American housing survey. http://www.census.gov/hhes/www/housing/ahs/ahs.html. (July 1, 2008).

U.S. Census Bureau. 2005b. Cartographic boundary files. http://www.census.gov/geo/www/cob/tr2000.html. (June 16, 2009).

U.S. Census Bureau. 2006a. Design and methodology: American community survey. Tech. Pap. 67. Washington, DC: U.S. Government Printing Office. 420 p.

U.S. Census Bureau. 2006b. State and county QuickFacts. http://quickfacts.census.gov/qfd/states/00000.html. (September 3, 2008).

U.S. Department of Agriculture, Forest Service [USDA FS]. 1999. Wood handbook—wood as an engineering material. Gen. Tech. Rep. FPL-GTR-113. Madison, WI: Forest Products Laboratory. 463 p.

Wilson, P.L.; Funck, J.W.; Avery, R.B. 1987. Fuelwood characteristics of northwestern conifers and hardwoods. Res. Bul. 60. Corvallis, OR: Oregon State University, College of Forestry, Forest Research Lab. 42 p.

www.ingramcontent.com/pod-product-compliance
Lightning Source LLC
Chambersburg PA
CBHW081136280526
45787CB00007B/3109